FURRY FRIENDS

Project Book

Learn how to create a
collection of furry friends

5 projects inside

Welcome to the wonderful world of Needle Felting!

This kit has been specifically designed for adults only.

Learning a new skill is always exciting – we're here to help you get started. Needle felting is a great way to relax. It is created by agitating the fibres of the wool with a barbed needle, which then transforms the wool into a solid shape or wool sculpture.

So, what can you make with needle felting? Well, anything your imagination lets you. The most popular creations are animals and birds, but there really are no limits. It's your creation, big, small, classic or experimental. It is your journey to decide and enjoy!

This kit provides everything you need to make your very own Needle Felt Dog or Cat. Whichever you choose to make, you can adjust the instructions to create the other one at a later time.

There are also three other options, each with a step-by-step guide for you to try. Don't think of the instructions as rules. You may discover ways that work better for you, so let your imagination run wild.

Remember, every skill takes effort to master, so don't be disheartened if it's not perfect the first time. The most important thing is that you have fun and enjoy yourself.

Let's start your Needle Felting journey!

KIT CONTENTS

WHAT'S INCLUDED:

- Roving yarn
- Felt needle
- Foam block
- Plastic safety eyes

WHAT IS FELTING?

Felting is when you combine the fibres/hair by using a felting needle to interlock, therefore creating a matted fabric. The more you stab into the felt, the more compressed the fabric becomes and solid the design will be.

THE BASICS OF FELTING

Traditionally, needle felting is done with sheep's wool from various breeds such as Corriedale, Teeswater and most commonly Merino. Alternative wools can be used as you get more skilled, such as alpaca, angora, mohair and yak.

If you're vegan, there are other fibres available to use, such as bamboo.

When the wool is stabbed with the felting needle, it pulls the wool together. As you keep turning and stabbing the wool over and over, it pulls the wool into itself, creating a firm shape.

One of the advantages of needle felting, is that an error can be fixed by either adding more wool, or continuing to poke the wool until you are happy with the end result.

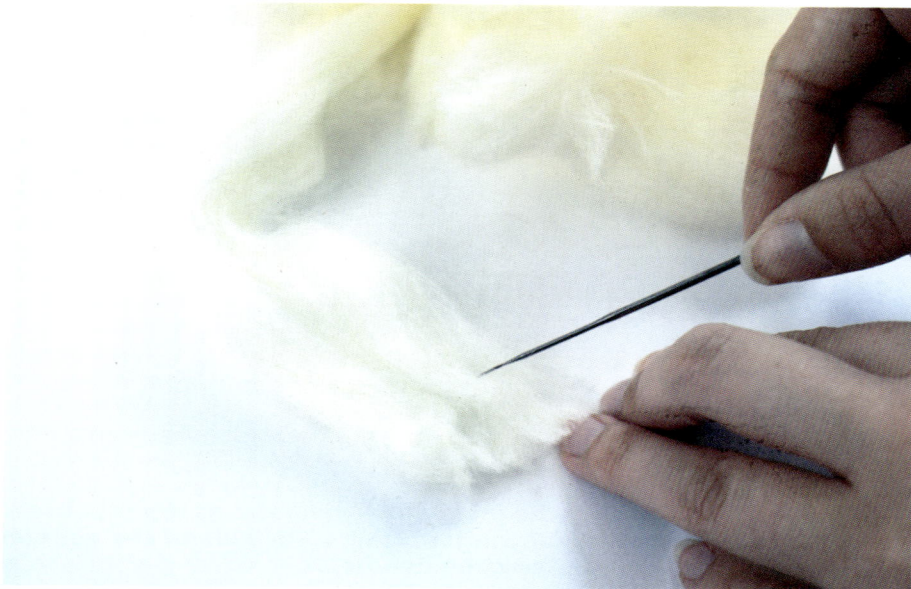

NEEDLE FELTING EQUIPMENT THE BASICS:

The process of moving the needle in and out of the wool is called poking or stabbing. To begin with, the needle supplied in this kit is a good all-rounder. When you get more accomplished and your creations get more advanced, there are different needles to use - from a very fine point (higher number) to very coarse point (lower number).

THE TRIANGLE POINTED NEEDLES:

The triangle pointed needles have three sides at the point with notches or barbs along each side.

THE #36 TRIANGLE POINT:

The #36 triangle point is most commonly used for coarse wool and faster felting. It leaves larger holes in the wool, this means you have to go over the punched surface with a finer needle if you want to hide them.

THE #38 TRIANGLE NEEDLE:

The #38 triangle needle is a great all-rounder needle.

THE #40 TRIANGLE NEEDLE:

The #40 triangle needle is used for fine details such as sculpting faces.

THE STAR POINT NEEDLE:

The star point needle has 4 sides of notches or barbs. Having one extra side, this needle is excellent for faster fine felting.

There are also multi needle tools available to hold 3-25 needles for completing larger scale projects.

Note: Always hold the needle just below the bend at the top. Do not apply pressure with your finger against the side of the needle at an angle or you could break the needle.

FOAM PAD:

This item helps you to protect your crafting surface and your fingers while you needle the felt.

WOOL ROVING:

This is wool that has been washed and combed, usually through a carding (like combing) machine. When carded, the wool goes in the same direction, making it easier to felt with. When separating the wool, always pull gently and never cut with scissors. Always leave some spare wool on makes in case you need to add more on.

WOOL BATTING:

This is wool that has not been combed or carded and is coarser than a roving. It's good to use as a core wool for creating shapes. It is also cheaper to buy than wool roving. Use this for the bulk of your creation, then add the wool roving or coloured wool.

OTHER ITEMS:

You can also use other craft items with your felt creations such as craft eyes, wire, pipe cleaners, whiskers, accessories like clothes or props.

Use your creativity and your new skill to add to this list and give more character to your furry friends!

WARNINGS!

All the makes included in this book are designed specifically for adults.

When working with needles ensure you keep them in a safe place. Never put pins in your mouth or stick them in your clothes. Keep all needlework in the packaging when not working.

Keep the sharp end of the needle away from you and your eyes at all times.

Keep all contents out of the reach of children.

DOG

DOG

Use the kit to make mans best friend. You won't be able to stop yourself falling in love this friendly guy.

YOU WILL NEED

· Roving yarn
· Felt needle
· Foam block
· Plastic safety eyes

METHOD

1. Begin by arranging your wool, needle, craft eyes and foam pad onto a cleared and hard surface.

2. Separate your cream wool into sections. A large one for the body, a smaller one for the head and then 6 equal amounts for the legs, 1 ear and tail, and a smaller section for the snout.

3. Separate the brown wool into a piece the same size as the cream for the second dog ear.

4. Take your large piece of wool and roll it into the shape of your dog.

5. Place it on the foam block, grab your needle and start poking the wool - you don't have to go too deep. Keep turning the wool as you poke, so it firms up all over and prevents the fibres sticking to the foam block. Keep poking the wool until you are happy.

6. Repeat the same process for the head.

7. Take your smaller pieces of cream and brown wool and roll into a sausage shape. Work on one at a time and shape into the legs, ears and tail.

8. Take the smaller section for the snout and poke this until you get a firm snout.

9. Attach the snout to the head. Now for the fun part! Putting all the parts together.

10. Start with the head and body. Place them together on your foam block, and with the needle vertical but straight, go through the body into the head.

11. Repeat the same process for each body part.

12. Add a small bit of black wool to the snout for the nose.

13. Once it's all attached together, add the brown wool to the tail.

14. Now add the spots – to do this, get small sections of brown wool and gently poke into the body until attached.

15. Make two holes on the face for the eyes and gently screw them in. This can be tricky on first makes, but don't worry. You can use two small balls of black wool instead.

NOTES

Use the space below to make your own personal notes on the previous project to help when you come back to make it again!

CAT

CAT

Create this cuddly cat with your kit and be blown away by how simple it is to go from some felt to your new furry friend.

YOU WILL NEED

- Roving yarn
- Felt needle
- Foam block
- Plastic safety eyes

METHOD

1. Begin by arranging your wool, needle, craft eyes and foam pad onto a cleared and hard surface.

2. Separate your cream wool into sections. A large one for the body, a smaller one for the head and then 6 equal amounts for the legs, tail, and a smaller section for the snout.

3. Separate the brown wool into a piece the same size as the cream to make two brown triangle ears for the cat.

4. Take your large piece of wool and roll it into the shape of your cat's body, tucking in any loose ends.

5. Place it on the foam block, grab your needle and start poking the wool - you don't have to go too deep. Keep turning the wool as you poke, so it firms up all over and prevents the fibres sticking to the foam block. Keep poking the wool until you are happy.

6. Repeat the same process for the head.

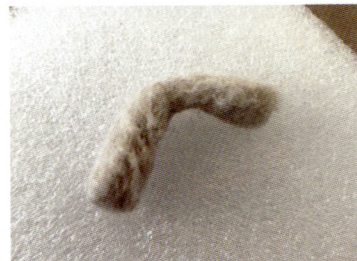

7. Take your smaller pieces of cream and brown wool and roll into a sausage shape. Work on one at a time and shape into the legs, ears and tail.

8. Take the smaller section for the snout and poke this until you get a firm snout.

9. Attach the snout to the head. Now for the fun part! Putting all the parts together.

10. Start with the head and body. Place them together on your foam block, and with the needle vertical but straight, go through the body into the head.

11. Repeat the same process for each body part.

12. Add a small bit of black wool to the snout for the nose.

13. Once it's all attached together, add the brown wool to the tail.

14. Now add the spots – to do this, get small sections of brown wool and gently poke into the body until attached.

15. Make two holes on the face for the eyes and gently screw them in. This can be tricky on first makes, but don't worry. You can use two small balls of black wool instead.

NOTES

Use the space below to make your own personal notes on the previous project to help when you come back to make it again!

CUTE MOUSE

MOUSE

This adorable little mouse is sure to bring a smile to yours and other faces, whether gifted or kept as your own little friend.

YOU WILL NEED

· Wool Roving
· Cream or White Wool
· Pink Wool
· Plastic eyes or (Black Wool)
· Whiskers
· Foam board
· Triangle pointed needle

METHOD

1. Start by separating the white wool. You will need a large part for the body and a smaller one for the head.

2. Roll both parts into a pear shape. Once firm, attach them together.

3. Roll two pieces of white wool to make the arms.

4. Add two small pieces of pink wool onto the ends, then attach the arms onto the body.

5. Take your pink wool and make four balls. Pinch two of the balls together at the bottom to create an ear shape. Attach them to the head.

6. Flatten the other two balls of pink wool to make the feet. Attach to the white wool at the bottom.

7. To finish, use a small ball of pink wool for the nose. With your needle, poke a line across to indent wool for the mouth and add the eyes.

8. You can finish with whiskers (optional). How wonderful! Your very own little mouse.

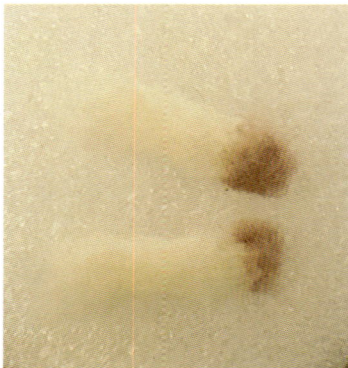

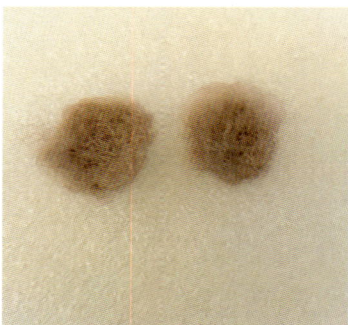

NOTES

Use the space below to make your own personal notes on the previous project to help when you come back to make it again!

RABBIT

RABBIT

Make this friendly rabbit, just make sure to watch out for your carrots!

YOU WILL NEED
· Core Wool or Cream Wool
· Brown/Chestnut Wool or colour of
  choice for Rabbit
· Blue Wool
· Pink Wool
· Black Wool
· Plastic Eyes or (Black Wool)
· Scissors/Snips

METHOD

1. Sepcrate your choice of wool into sections for the body, head, ears, arms and legs.

2. Starting with the body, add a section of cream wool to the front. Repeat this for the ears.

3. Roll the wool for the legs into two sausage shapes. When they start to firm, add the white wool shaped into a foot.

4. Attach the legs to the body.

5. Next, make the head and attach the ears.

6. Take a small section of white for the neck by rolling into a sausage shape and attach to the body.

7. Add cream wool to the bottom of the face and a small bit of pink wool for the nose.

8. To add the line under the nose, get a slither of black wool, roll in your fingers to form a thread – dampening your fingers may help the shaping process. Gently poke into place and attach the head to the neck.

9. Begin making the scarf. Take your blue wool and shape into an oblong - poke at the edges until it forms a rectangle.

10. Once firm, take your scissors/snips and carefully cut the ends as pictured to make it look like a scarf - check the scarf fits around the neck before cutting!
If it does not yet fit, add wool or keep poking to get the right fit.

11. When the scarf is complete, wrap around the neck. Poke where the two ends meet to attach together.

12. Finish off by adding your eyes, either plastic or wool.

Well Done! A beautiful Rabbit to keep for yourself or gift to another.

NOTES

Use the space below to make your own personal notes on the previous project to help when you come back to make it again!

BUDGIE

BUDGIE

This colourful budgie could be yours by following the steps in the next few pages

YOU WILL NEED

- Wool Roving
- Core Wool
- Blue Wool
- White Wool
- Brown Wool
- Yellow Wool
- Black Wool
- Plastic eyes (or Black Wool)

METHOD

1. Using core wool, shape the budgies body.

2. Once firm, add your blue wool on top, leaving some uncovered as white for the head.

3. Now, get two small bits of brown wool for the legs. Roll them into an arch shape and poke till firm.

4. Make your wings, and add black zig zag lines.

5. Roll a small piece of yellow wool into the shape of a beak and poke until firm and attach to the face.

6. Then add a small piece of blue wool on top of the beak.

7. Attach the legs.

8. To complete your budgie, add the eyes. Then, get three small pieces of black wool and add to each side of the face.
Well done! What a cute little creation.

44

NOTES

Use the space below to make your own personal notes on the
previous project to help when you come back to make it again!